THE
NEIGHBORHOOD
TUTORING
PROGRAM

THE
NEIGHBORHOOD
TUTORING
PROGRAM

A Guide for Establishing a Neighborhood Tutoring Program
for Your Church or Civic Organization

DUANE M. MILLER

WESTBOW
PRESS®
A DIVISION OF THOMAS NELSON
& ZONDERVAN

WestBow Press books may be ordered through booksellers or by contacting:

WestBow Press
A Division of Thomas Nelson & Zondervan
1663 Liberty Drive
Bloomington, IN 47403
www.westbowpress.com
1 (866) 928-1240

ISBN: 978-1-5127-0221-7 (sc)
ISBN: 978-1-5127-1997-0 (hc)
ISBN: 978-1-5127-0222-4 (e)

Print information available on the last page.

WestBow Press rev. date: 12/10/2015

This book is dedicated to the glory of God. Without His urging through the Holy Spirit, the Neighborhood Tutoring Program would still be a figment of man's imagination, and this book would be but a distant dream. I also would be very remiss if I did not recognize the critical support provided by many people. First and foremost, I want to recognize and thank Lynn, Avis, Terri Lynn, and Laura for their review and proofreading of the book and for their many valuable suggestions on ways to enhance the manuscript. Lastly, I want to thank my dear and loving wife, Gayle, for her patient encouragement throughout this challenging project.

Neighborhood Tutoring Program (NTP)

A neighborhood-oriented, volunteer-based program designed
to assist students living in economically disadvantaged
environments by providing a source of free tutoring in
all academic subjects from grades one through ten.

Publication

The Neighborhood Tutoring Program (NTP)

Edition One

Author: Duane M. Miller

The mission of the NTP project is twofold: first,
to establish and operate Neighborhood Tutoring
Centers in the DC metropolitan area, and second,
to assist churches and other service-oriented
organizations across the county to establish volunteer-
based tutoring centers in their neighborhoods.

The Neighborhood Tutoring Program was
written to help meet the mission of the
Neighborhood Tutoring Program (NTP).

The NTP project is a dream come true for the author and
a work accomplished for the glory and honor of God.

Remember, we are commanded to "Love one another.
As I have loved you, so you must love one another.
By this all men will know that you are my disciples,
if you love one another" (John 13:34–35 NIV).

For further information about the
NTP, contact the following:

Duane M. Miller, tel: 703-743-1974
E-mail: Dmiller832@comcast.net

The Neighborhood Tutoring Program (NTP) Guide for Establishing Neighborhood Tutoring Programs

Contents

Foreword

The Neighborhood Tutoring Program

The Neighborhood Tutoring Program (NTP) is the realization of a dream nurtured in my mind during many years of teaching middle school mathematics and social studies in economically disadvantaged suburban neighborhoods. During this period, I annually observed a group of students who obviously needed additional academic assistance but did not have the resources or the wherewithal to obtain the needed assistance through existing channels. By channels, I mean such programs as for-pay tutoring, afterschool tutoring programs, and other community-based programs physically housed outside of the needy neighborhoods.

Over time, I became convinced that the academic assistance needed to be brought to the neighborhoods instead of trying to get the neighborhood to come to the academic assistance! This realization, in turn, begged the question, just how can we take the tutoring where it is needed?

My solution was to establish onsite, volunteer-based tutoring programs sponsored by neighborhood churches or other civic-minded organizations. My two major goals for these onsite programs are to, first, provide students the needed academic assistance, and second, offer volunteers the rich emotional and spiritual rewards that come from helping a neighbor in need. These were initially and continue to be ambitious goals!

I chose to develop a model tutoring program that was funded strictly with donations, relied on no federal or state financial support, could be easily tailored to fit individual community needs, and could be easily transported from one community to another. The Neighborhood Tutoring Program model is the child of these dreams. The model that I developed has been validated through several tutoring programs that have been established in a variety of neighborhood environments.

The basic onsite volunteer-based NTP model is documented in this book. My intention in writing the book is to provide a clear, concise blueprint that others can employ to develop their own onsite tutoring programs. However, along with the blueprint comes an offer of free support to help new sponsors get their program established and operating. Like the basic NTP model, the assistance I offer through the NTP is flexible and tailored to the needs of the individual church or civic sponsor.

My dream is that the NTP will eventually lead to numerous neighborhood tutoring programs operating in hundreds of economically disadvantaged neighborhoods across the country.

Duane M. Miller
Founder, The Neighborhood Tutoring Program

Guide for Establishing Neighborhood Tutoring Programs

The purpose of this book is to provide a guide for establishing a volunteer-based tutoring center in your neighborhood. When using the term *neighborhood tutoring program* (NTP), I am referring to the specific program I offer to you. This program consists of this guide and a promise of personal assistance available to you. This assistance will be available over some mutually agreed upon timeframe during which you will establish and begin to operate your own tutoring center. When referring to your center, I will call it a tutoring center or tutoring center program. Each program a customer establishes should be tailored to meet the specific objectives and needs of the community being served and the desires of those establishing the program. There are, however, many topics that will likely come up while planning any tutoring center. This guide will reduce your learning curve in these relatively common areas.

This guide is arranged by topic, but the topics are not addressed in any critical or even chronological order. The reader might find it beneficial to first scan the book to become familiar with the content. Then, as you begin to plan your center, you can return to relevant sections and use them as a more specific planning guide or as a set of do's and don'ts for each aspect of the center.

1. Philosophy Behind the Neighborhood Tutoring Program (NTP) Concept

A. Take the Assistance to the Student

There may be several free or for-pay tutoring programs available in a community. In many cases, however, students living in lower-income neighborhoods may not have access to these resources due to limited funds, lack of transportation, and other factors. The NTP is based on the premise that tutoring support needs to be taken to the students in economically depressed neighborhoods rather than to expect students to come to the source of tutoring.

B. Academic Goal

The academic goal for the NTP is twofold: 1. Assist students with homework and review, and reinforce skills currently being addressed in the regular classroom. 2. Once the first goal is met during a tutoring session, shift to review and reinforcement of skills addressed earlier in the academic year or to skills for which the student requires reinforcement.

C. Volunteer Staffing

Another premise is that the NTP will be staffed by volunteers. Therefore, the program must be structured in a manner that meets volunteer needs for flexibility while still supporting program goals and meeting student needs.

D. NTP Supplements and Reinforces Other Schools

It must be understood that a tutoring center is not a school. The neighborhood tutoring center will support a much larger educational effort within a student's life. It is very important to keep this relationship in mind as you plan and build your

NTP. If you structure your tutoring center to be an island unto itself, it will likely become just that, and probably to the detriment of your students!

E. Funding

Funding for the NTP is not dictated or even discussed in depth in this guide. In some cases, the tutoring center might be funded by grant monies. In other cases, the sponsoring organization or donations will fund the center. Regardless of how your center is funded, it is important you include funding in your planning process.

2. Sponsorship and Purpose of Your Program

It is important to identify the purpose of your tutoring program and who will sponsor the program. This might seem like a simple matter; after all, we just want to tutor students! However, I suggest you slow down and think it through.

A. Sponsorship

As I discuss development of tutoring centers, I will use the term *sponsorship* to identify the organization that develops and operates the tutoring center. In other words, it is the organization that causes tutoring to occur in an organized manner by pulling together all the needed resources, identifying and training volunteers, attracting students to partake in the services offered, and finally, guiding and directing operations of the tutoring center. Many different organizations can fulfill the roles just outlined. The type of organization that steps forward will, to some degree, impact center operations. I make this statement with the knowledge that tutoring centers sponsored by the NTP have three basic parts: a character-building opening session, homework assistance, and some form of remedial and reinforcement assistance. The first of these will be most affected by the organization that sponsors the center. For example, if your sponsor is a church, emphasis during your character-building sessions might be on various issues encountered in the Christian faith. If a parent-teacher association (PTA) sponsors a tutoring center, the focus of the character-building session might be oriented toward good citizenship, proper behavior and attitudes in school, and so forth. If the sponsor is a community service organization, such as a Lion's Club or Rotary Club, the character-building session might emphasize values of their respective programs they believe worthy of being passed on to the students.

B. Purpose

So what is the purpose of your program? This may seem like a very simple question. But I suggest you give this question careful consideration. Carefully consider what services to focus your efforts on and realize that this decision will affect all your planning and organizational efforts. Without adequate focus, resources for the tutoring center program might quickly be dissipated on useful activities that, unfortunately, do not help to accomplish the primary purpose of the program. For example, without focus, a new tutoring program might emphasize mentoring, which is admirable but also clearly different than tutoring. As another example, you might be asked to provide English as a Second Language (ESL) instruction within your center, which would be admirable, but will you have the necessary resources to support both a tutoring and an ESL program? I believe it is far wiser to focus your resources on the primary purpose established for the center than to provide several services, none of which are adequately resourced or delivered. If you start out with a clear and limited focus, you always have the option of expanding your services to other areas in the future. It's better to be good at your main thing than to be mediocre at several services, impressing no one in the process!

C. Christian Sponsorship

The NTP started as a ministry sponsored by a local church. Thus, tutoring centers that have been established and are operated by the NTP are sponsored by this same church. So for purposes of providing an example, how has this sponsorship affected these centers? First, the church in this case has many outreach ministries and, therefore, has been a valuable source of advice on a wide assortment of issues regarding establishment and conduct of a faith-based ministry. Second, the church has established policies and procedures that are to be followed; these provided a structure within which the NTP was framed. Additionally, the sponsoring church has a clearly stated mission, which is to bring the message of Jesus Christ to the secular environment around the church. Therefore, one of the stated purposes of the NTP-operated tutoring centers is to represent the person and message of Jesus Christ within the supported neighborhoods. And finally, this framework directly affects the content of the character-building portion of each tutoring session and serves as an overall guide for tutor attitudes and behavior throughout the tutoring sessions.

D. Sponsorship by Secular Organizations

Most, or probably all, sponsoring organizations will have policies, procedures, and expectations that will partially shape development and operation of their tutoring centers. And I fully recognize that some sponsoring organizations are likely to have a more direct impact on the structure and organization than will other organizations. As with all topics addressed in this document, every tutoring center will have its own unique personality. This personality should be the result of decisions made by all stakeholders to best meet the purpose, goals, objectives, and operating constraints of each center.

E. So Where Does the NTP Fit In?

Your question now might be just where the NTP fits into the development of your tutoring center. The mission of the NTP, again, is twofold: 1. Establish and operate tutoring centers. 2. Provide information and assistance to other organizations that choose to establish and operate a neighborhood tutoring center. Once developed, the tutoring center and program will belong to the sponsoring organization, not to the NTP, and will be operated by the sponsoring organization, not by the NTP. Advice and assistance provided by the NTP will consist of this publication and ongoing verbal assistance as the centers are planned and developed. NTP support may not have a definite deadline; neither is it expected to extend indefinitely. The timeframe of support will be as mutually agreed on by myself (the NTP) and the customer.

3. Selecting a Tutoring Center Facility

Once you have identified the neighborhood you plan to support, you need to identify a location where the tutoring center can be established. Location, location, and location are key! Remember, one of the goals of your tutoring center program is to offer onsite tutoring. *Onsite* means onsite! If most of your students live in one housing development or in housing developments in close proximity to each other, a community room might be an excellent choice for a location. If such a facility is not available, search for a business or civic organization that might be willing to donate space in the immediate area of the targeted neighborhood. Keep in mind that the tutoring center can be set up and taken down for each session, and storage space (a few small folding tables, chairs, maybe a filing cabinet and a closet for storing supplies, etc.) would be minimal.

An important but perhaps less obvious reason to identify space is to cultivate relationships with people in pivotal positions. For example, if you hope to use a community room in a housing development, you need to sell yourself and your program to the property management company that controls those spaces. If you must turn to sources outside of the housing development, then carefully cultivate relationships with the people having power to grant access to the desired spaces. I believe that you will find the mission of your onsite tutoring program easy to explain and quickly and strongly supported! This should be a real ally for you when seeking a home for your center! Take heart and start searching for the needed space!

4. Clients

One of the first tasks when planning a tutoring center is to identify your student body. First, what community or neighborhood do you plan to serve? Is there a particular group in the neighborhood school environment that you want to serve? Perhaps there is a group within No Child Left Behind that you believe needs tutoring service. What grade levels are you planning to serve? What subjects will you tutor— academic subjects (to include core subjects such as reading, writing, language arts, math, science, social science); specialty subjects (e.g. music, art, industrial arts); all subjects? How you answer these questions will have implications for space requirements, required skill levels of your volunteers and the material resources that you will need.

5. Level of Tutoring Support

What depth and frequency of support do you plan to offer? Will you tutor five days a week, just on weekends, or some other plan? What time will you conduct the tutoring sessions? Will you provide just homework help or is your goal to move beyond this level of assistance to address remedial needs of students? Or perhaps you will choose to also provide reinforcement and extension of existing skills. Another issue to consider is the role that computers will play in your program. Will your program be totally hardcopy based, or will there be some hardcopy and some computer support? If you plan to use computers, you will probably want internet access, which raises the issue of funding. A further consideration should be whether or not you will have a tutoring center library. And, if you have a library, will it be designed for tutor support only or for both tutors and students? When considering the above issues, I strongly recommend a threefold approach for your tutoring program:

A. Character Building and Self-Image

Considering the background of some of the students who may be in your program, character building and reinforcement of self-image might be important goals. Students need to know that they are loved, that they are okay, and that they are supported by the tutors regardless of what their academic performance has previously been. These character-building and self-esteem elements, like everything in the educational process, need to be planned and evaluated. I strongly suggest you devote a specific amount of time at the beginning of each session to these character-building issues. Content of these sessions will depend upon the overall objective of your tutoring program, the materials you can provide, and the experience and training of the tutorial staff.

B. Homework Assistance

I recommend you assist students by focusing on their homework, reviewing tests that have been returned, and so forth. This approach will provide an easy but valid methodology to review and reinforce skills and also to provide students an opportunity to rather quickly see improvement in their daily performance.

This, in turn, offers a confidence builder for students who have not had much academic success and, as a result, do not feel good about themselves or their academic abilities. Building confidence for these students should be high on the priority list when establishing goals for your Neighborhood Tutoring Program! (Refer to attachment I-4 for additional comments regarding online homework assistance.)

C. Reinforcement and Extension

Be bold and move beyond homework assistance! If you accept this as a goal, I strongly recommend that you shape your program to reinforce skills previously addressed in the student's regular classroom. Accomplishing this goal will take some careful planning and a lot of hard work! The neat thing is that essentially all public and private school systems operate within a well-defined curriculum that is carefully paced throughout the academic year. By working closely with the supported school system, it is possible to select topics for review and reinforcement (i.e., what you do beyond homework help) in the tutoring center that closely parallels regular classroom instruction.

In fact, if positive relationships are developed with the supported school system, it is quite possible that access will be granted to a variety of materials that you could apply in your tutoring center. Remember, your goal should be to reinforce material, not to throw an entirely new curriculum at your students! I recommend that you plan to address materials approximately one or two weeks behind the time they were covered in the supported school. In this manner, you will avoid occasionally getting ahead of the school's pacing, which is a recipe for frustrating students! By working slightly behind the school's pacing, your tutoring center will provide an extremely valuable service: reviewing and reinforcing recently addressed materials. Practice and repetition are an excellent way to increase long-term retention; the tutoring center program can provide a valuable service by supplementing the amount of time available for reinforcement in the regular school setting.

As the spring semester moves along, you will need to decide how much emphasis will be placed on preparation for state- or federal-mandated testing. Students who have mandated testing (called standards of learning—SOL—tests in some states) will spend considerable classroom time preparing for these tests. You might want to coordinate with the supported school system to determine whether or not additional preparation time in the tutoring center is good use of your limited tutoring hours. If you choose to supplement preparation time allocated in the school, be aware that there are many excellent online sites (refer to attachment II-12) that offer materials. One of these sources will likely be a local state website that addresses test preparation, possibly including released tests from previous years. If desired, these sites would also offer excellent material to address end of year test taking strategies.

D. Tutoring Center Library

The question of a library is essentially two-tiered. First, what type of resources will you have for tutors to use if they need assistance or desire to review methods used in the school curriculum? As a minimum, tutors should have access to teachers' editions of the basic textbooks students are using in their classrooms. Accessing these textbooks could take any of several forms. If you are very lucky or persuasive, you might try asking the supported school system for copies. Another source could be the textbook companies from whom the school system is purchasing their textbooks. And, of course, there is always the possibility of purchasing copies of the textbooks either from the textbook company or from an online source such as Amazon or eBay.

In addition to textbooks, tutors should have access to a basic set of classroom books such as dictionaries, thesauruses, basic reference books (math, science, social studies, language arts) and others as the need becomes apparent. Again, many of these resources can be acquired from used book outlets or online resources for a fraction of their new cost.

Students also need books! Students should be expected to bring their basic textbooks to the tutoring sessions. They should also bring classroom handouts with which they need assistance. However, some schools do not issue textbooks for home use. Therefore, the tutoring center must be prepared to provide access to these texts to support the basic tutoring mission. One avenue for access might be online through the textbook companies. Many companies provide extremely useful resources online and free of charge. In addition, textbook companies usually provide online resources for a fee. In almost every case, there will be a parent's support section included within the textbook company's online resources. It would be useful to ensure your tutors are aware of these resources.

Another issue regarding the tutoring center library is general reading material and books. Do you plan to acquire an assortment of reading books, especially for elementary students? If so, will these books be available to sign out, and if so, for how long? If you decide to have a reading library, how will you acquire the books? Again, there are many potential sources. Asking for donations is usually a productive process! Often elementary books can be purchased from used book outlets or online resources for very reasonable charges. Local libraries also have periodic book sales.

6. Staffing the Tutoring Center

As you plan for your tutoring center, you must consider whether you have adequate resources from which to draw volunteers with the requisite background skills. Where will you turn to recruit these volunteers, and how will you conduct your recruitment program? Is there an organizational structure (school system, church, PTA, etc.) through which you can contact potential volunteers? Have you done any preliminary surveying of your target volunteers to judge the response you can expect to receive? How long will you expect your volunteers to commit to the tutoring program—a year, two years, a semester? Are there adequate resources to recruit replacements as you experience a normal turnover of volunteers? Following are some specific issues you should consider when staffing the tutoring center.

A. Number of Volunteers Needed

The number of volunteers needed will, of course, be driven by the space limitations of the tutoring center and the number of students your program attracts. In addition, whether the center uses one-on-one tutoring or has tutors working with multiple students will influence the number of tutors needed. Obviously, one-on-one tutoring will require the same number of tutors and students. If your operating concept calls for tutors to work simultaneously with more than one student, I strongly recommend that you plan on assigning two and definitely no more than three students to each tutor. Assigning an excessive number of students to a tutor will quickly limit the individual service that the tutor can provide and, in effect, severely reduce the quality of the support envisioned for your tutoring program. Remember, one of the goals of your tutoring program should be to reduce the relatively high student-teacher ratio that usually exists in a classroom setting.

B. Required skills

The required skill set for the tutors will be driven partially by the mission of the center. If you intend to function basically as a homework assistance center, then the tutor skill set will be somewhat less than if you intend to delve more deeply into teaching and reinforcing skills. Generally speaking, the deeper you expect your tutors to go in teaching and reinforcing skills, the more experience the staff should have. However, from a practical standpoint, you will probably have tutors with a wide mixture of teaching and other professional and technical background experiences. As a rough estimate, we recommend a ratio of at least two tutors with some teaching or classroom experience for each tutor with no teaching or classroom experience. In addition to background experience, the mix of tutors recruited (i.e., by academic area or specialties) should parallel the subjects to be tutored in the center. It is important to assign students to tutors having adequate expertise in the subject area in which the student is seeking assistance. Students can be easily discouraged and lose interest in tutoring if they feel the assistance being offered is not solid or the tutor lacks confidence in his or her own ability.

C. Sources of Volunteers

The first source of volunteers might well be the organization sponsoring the tutoring center. If the sponsoring organization cannot provide an adequate number of the desired mix of tutors, then seek volunteers elsewhere or reduce the goal for the number of students to be tutored. There are several sources that could be tapped for tutors. One might be public or private school systems serving the community where the tutoring center is located. Other sources might be civic organizations, churches, and active adult communities. The imagination of the planners is the only limiting factor when seeking sources for recruiting tutors!

D. Training of Volunteers

The topics and depth of material to be addressed in your training program obviously will be dependent on the structure of your program. However, for starters, you should have an orientation session for all new tutors and receptionists at the start of each semester (assumes at least some new tutors or receptionists the second semester) and at least one information/ training session for all tutors and receptionists at the beginning of each academic year. Examples of topics to be discussed in the sessions are addressed in the following paragraphs. In each case, the topics are examples and are not meant to be all inclusive.

1) New Tutor/Receptionist Orientation. Attachment II-9 is an outline that I have used for new tutor orientations at NTP-operated tutoring centers. We suggest you ask yourself the following questions when planning content for your new tutor and receptionist orientation session:

a) What do the tutors and receptionists need to know to perform their roles in a manner that is safe, legal, and in accordance with the established tutoring program's mission and procedures?

b) Are the tutors and receptionists familiar with the educational environment, particularly in regard to the privacy act, definitions for child abuse, requirements for reporting the same, acceptable behavior and speech in the educational environment, and so forth? These topics might seem very basic to individuals with educational backgrounds. However, they may be foreign to a tutor who has never worked in a school setting. Considering how easy it is to get in legal trouble in an educational environment, I strongly recommend you come down on the side of safety for your tutors when planning content. Therefore, don't hesitate to address any and all topics that help to fully prepare your tutors. Remember, it is far better to initially err on the side of caution than to find yourself addressing a serious situation after the fact.

c) What publications (e.g., forms used in the center, operating procedure handbook) should the new tutors and receptionists be familiar with in order to fully perform their assigned tasks?

d) What specific expectations are there for tutors and receptionists? Are these clearly stated in some publication which is known and available to the staff?

2). Annual Information Session. Topics covered in the annual review should include changes to policies, procedures, expectations, and documentation from the previous academic year. Specific topics need to be determined by the center management who are in the position to know what changes have been made or are expected to be implemented in the coming academic year.

3). Periodic Communications. A third form of training, in the broad sense, is keeping volunteers informed of ongoing procedural changes and events throughout the academic year. Certainly word of mouth is one method for this communication! However, you might also consider a more formal process. One way that has worked well in NTP tutoring centers is to publish a newsletter periodically throughout the year. This newsletter might be as brief as a short e-mail sent out to volunteers, or it could be made as "newsy" as you and your volunteer staff desire. One example of a newsletter is included in attachment II-10.

7. Ties with the Supported Community School System(s)

One of the basic questions that must be addressed when establishing your tutoring center program is the relationship you wish to establish with the community schools serving your students. If your decision is none, then there is no need to establish these ties! However, you will likely find that your tutoring efforts are more effective if they align closely with the academic curriculums and activities the students are exposed to on a daily basis.

I highly recommended that you determine which schools (public and private) the students in the targeted neighborhood attend. If you are fortunate, most of your potential students will feed into one elementary, one middle, and one high school. This situation would make coordination far simpler for you. On the other hand, if you find that your potential students feed into a variety of schools, you have a much greater challenge! In this case, you might want to initially limit the neighborhood you support. Then, once your tutoring center is operating smoothly, you might choose to increase the number of neighborhoods served and thereby the number of schools involved. This approach would simplify initial startup for your tutoring center.

Reaching out to neighborhood schools will also facilitate communication between volunteers in your tutoring program and professionals in the school systems. It is important that this communication link be established and nurtured. Not only will positive communications facilitate day-to-day operations in your tutoring program, it will also go a long way toward avoiding potential hard feelings or conflicts between the two groups of professional educators. By reaching out to and sincerely attempting to maintain communications with the school staff, you will in effect be saying, "We want to work with you as part of one comprehensive team with a single common goal: to provide our students the best possible program that we can jointly deliver!"

When you reach out to the supported school system, I suggest you begin by researching how the school system is structured and how it operates. For example, in some school systems your tutoring program might be viewed as an outside community activity with which school staff lacks the authority to interact. In these cases, interaction with the supported school becomes a legal issue that needs to be addressed; simply getting irritated with the school staff for "refusing to work with your center" will yield nothing but frustration and hard feelings! Most large school systems will have an office that develops school–business partnerships. It is likely that you will need to work with that office to determine with whom you should work and what documentation is needed to facilitate the desired interaction. It might take some time and effort to develop this partnership agreement, but once in place, the partnership agreements will make it far easier for you to interact with the schools.

In other school systems, you might find that the appropriate first stop would be to introduce yourself and your program to the principal and to the head of the guidance department. Not only would this approach demonstrate respect for the management structure within the school system, it would also provide an entry point through which you can contact other staff members in the school. In reality, it is easy to turn to a school website, check out their curriculum, and get the names of teachers and contact them directly. However, I strongly recommend against this approach. Keep in mind that schools are entities having their own unique cultures, and there are legal guidelines that must be followed by you and the school staff! To try to go around or to ignore these norms is to insult the school professionals, which can never be in your best interest! I strongly recommend that you take the time to understand and respectfully follow appropriate procedures—it will certainly be to your gain!

8. Legal Requirements

Research state and local laws as necessary to ensure you are meeting all legal requirements. Examples of items that need to be considered are the following:

A. Background Investigations

Your local government agencies will very likely require background investigations for volunteers working with underaged students. If background investigations are required, you will need to determine who will conduct the investigations for your tutoring program, how long will it take for each investigation to be completed, and what the cost will be for the investigations. If your sponsoring organization is a church, that entity probably has a program in place for conducting background investigations of the type you will need. Whether or not your tutoring program will be charged for the investigations will vary from case to case. If your sponsoring organization is something other than a church, they may or may not be familiar with obtaining background investigations. If they are not, I suggest you contact local law enforcement agencies to determine the appropriate path for you to follow. Also be sure to check whether the sponsoring organization (church, PTA, etc.) has additional requirements to which your tutoring program must adhere. These requirements could be of many types, but a common one could be periodic reporting of attendance data.

B. Liability Insurance

Keep in mind that the threat of lawsuits is very real, and the possibility for lawsuits arising out of tutoring center operations will be similar to that in a regular classroom. Also, keep in mind that many public school teachers feel the need to carry some form of liability insurance. With these factors as background, I strongly suggest your tutors be covered through some form of liability insurance. First, check to see whether or not the volunteers working in your tutoring program will have liability insurance coverage through the sponsoring organization. If so, you must determine whether or not there will be a cost for your tutoring program or for the individual volunteers.

If liability insurance is not provided, you must determine whether or not your tutoring program will provide the insurance coverage. If the decision is to provide liability insurance, the question becomes where to obtain the insurance and at what cost. In general, you can obtain this information from insurance companies that offer business insurance policies. As a start, most major insurance companies offer various forms of business insurance. Some of these business insurance policies will "fit" a faith-based, volunteer ministry and others may not. Some insurance companies cater to the needs of faith-based ministries. I will not recommend a specific insurance company, due to variations in requirements from state to state, but I will note that your local church or other local charity organizations should be good starting points to obtain this information.

C. Security

I recommend that you check with local law enforcement to determine what the security environment is in the general area of your tutoring center and to ensure that local security personnel are aware of your tutoring center. As a minimum, be sure to have the proper security contact information (names, telephone numbers, etc.) available and clearly posted for all tutor center personnel. Based on the conditions that exist, you must determine what procedures are needed to ensure safety for your tutors and students. For example, will you need parking passes? Should you arrange for tutor escorts to and from cars? Is the area notorious for drug trading activity? Also, while it is the responsibility of parents/guardians to escort their students to and from the tutoring center (paragraph 8F and attachment II-2), I strongly recommend that you determine whether or not it is safe to release a student from the tutoring center in the absence of a parent/guardian. As part of this safety consideration, be sure to have a clearly established, written policy (probably posted in your operational handbook: paragraph II-1) to cover handling of students who desire to depart from the tutoring center but do not have a parent/guardian or other identified escort present or available to contact.

D. Privacy Considerations

In most cases, your students will be under legal age. Therefore, it is very important that you and your staff are aware of legal issues and requirements regarding student privacy. This includes issues such as, but not limited to, establishing student records; contacting anyone regarding the student's performance or behavior in the tutoring center; and restrictions on providing advice to students, parents, or guardians on topics for which professional licenses are required. If you believe you need additional background information regarding the broad issue of student privacy, I recommend you contact the guidance department in one of your supported schools. Guidance personnel will be able to provide a wealth of knowledge on this subject or direct you to the sources with which you need to become familiar.

E. Volunteer and Student Behavior

Ensure that clear, specific guidance is provided to students and to the tutoring center staff regarding expected behavior in the tutoring center. Ensure that tutors are aware that their interactions with students are subject to state and federal law and that any violation of these laws could result in severe punishment, to include fines and imprisonment.

F. Parent/Guardian Consent and Expectations

A formal process needs to be implemented through which parents/guardians of underaged students give formal approval for their student(s) to participate in tutoring center activities (attachment II-2). As part of this process, I recommend that parents/guardians be given written guidance outlining their responsibilities toward their student(s) and toward the NTP. As part of these expectations, it should be made very clear that parents/guardians have sole responsibility for the safety and conduct of their students on the way to and from the tutoring center. Make it clear that the tutoring center has no responsibility for a student beyond the immediate confines of the tutoring center (attachment II-2).

9. NTP Management and Funding

You might have a great idea, but don't try going it on your own. It is important that a management framework be established for your tutoring program and that this occurs early in the development process.

A. Steering Committee

The steering committee should be a relatively small and flexible group that can meet as needed, offer advice, and make timely decisions. Not only will this group help surface issues that the day-to-day program manager may have overlooked, but they will also serve as a critical accountability group for the program. Membership on the committee will vary from center to center but as a minimum should include representatives of all of the major stakeholders in the program. For example, if your sponsoring organization is a church and you are targeting an economically depressed neighborhood, your steering committee might include representatives from groups such as: church leadership (pastor, elders etc.); church lay leadership; families residing within the target neighborhood; the supported public/private school system (e.g., elementary/middle/high school staff); and the housing development's management staff (if space they manage is being used for the tutoring center).

I recommend that the steering committee be chaired by the person who is essentially managing development of the tutoring center. This may well not be the person who ends up managing daily operations of the center; however, the first objective must be to get the center up and running. If this person believes he or she lacks the experience or time to chair the group, I recommend the steering committee be chaired by a person chosen for his or her program management experience and ability to work closely with the person managing day-to-day activities.

The frequency of steering committee meetings should be determined by the committee. I would expect that meetings would occur rather frequently (perhaps every two or three weeks) initially and then less often as the development progresses. I also recommend that the steering committee remain intact after the tutoring center becomes operational, with meetings quarterly or as otherwise desired by the committee.

B. Volunteers

Not all volunteers will have the time or the inclination to be involved in the management of the tutoring program. However, it is important to offer volunteers an opportunity to make suggestions or recommendations regarding tutoring center operations. One way to accomplish this could be to give volunteers an opportunity to attend and participate in steering committee meetings. Another method might be to publish steering committee meeting dates and involve volunteers in the setting of the agenda for those meetings. Another possibility might be to rotate volunteers through one or two positions on the steering committee. In any case, remember that you are operating with a volunteer staff and it is imperative that you keep your team united and supportive if your tutoring center is to succeed.

C. Funding

A neighborhood tutoring center is a relatively low-cost initiative, especially if donated space can be arranged. Most of the costs will come from basic educational supplies, student snacks, and teaching materials (e.g., textbooks, handouts, worksheets, electronic programs). For purposes of discussion, a very rough estimate of funding needs would be two hundred to three hundred dollars per semester once the tutoring center is set up and furnished. Given donated spaces, the major costs to initially furnish the tutoring center will be for small tables (number dependent upon the number of students), chairs, a filing cabinet, and possibly a book shelf for library materials. Again, a rough estimate of these costs would range from two to three hundred dollars, depending upon materials donated to the center, purchase of new or used furniture, and so forth. In any case, funding will not be a major issue for most organizations, and the amount spent can, to a degree, be tailored to match available funds. Having mentioned amounts, what might be likely sources of funding? The first source, of course, would be the sponsoring organization. Another source might be grants from any number of sources, including local, state, and federal governments. Another source of funding might be donations from community businesses and civic associations. Basically, funding can come from many sources; be creative and innovative in searching out possible avenues to obtain funds. To some degree, the funding of the tutoring center is limited only by the imagination of the planners!

10. Operational Issues

Depending upon the specific goals and nature of your tutoring program, there will be other topics upon which decisions are needed while structuring your program. Your steering committee and contacts at other neighborhood tutoring centers could help identify these issues. These issues may include:

A. Communication with Students (for inclement weather, etc.)

Some way to communicate with students should be established when the tutoring center is closed for unplanned reasons such as inclement weather. One rather easy way is to tie weather-based closures to a local school system. If the school system cancels activities, the center is closed.

B. Physical Setup in Center

Once your tutoring center becomes operational, the physical arrangement becomes an important issue. The physical layout of your tutoring center is important, although you may not have total control over this issue! For example, the space you are able to use may be one large open space or it may be a vacant apartment with several small rooms. Either situation can be made to work! However, in planning how to best use your space, keep in mind that you should avoid isolating a tutor in a room with students. This arrangement puts your tutor at increased risk if a student charges that improper behavior occurred. Secondly, as a policy, never allow students to remain in a room without a tutor or other staff member being present. This may seem like an overly cautious approach; however, as a rule of thumb, it is much easier to avoid problems than to recover from a problem! Additionally, assuming you do not have the luxury of one-on-one tutoring, you should plan for how groups will be structured. For example, will tutors be grouped with students by grade level, by subject matter, or in some combination of subject matter and grade level? Preplanning for this will avoid confusion at the tutoring center and will also clarify expectations for the volunteer tutors.

C. Student Records

Information maintained on student records could range from simple attendance records (e.g., sign-in and -out logs) to increasingly more detailed information such as student address, parent names, telephone numbers, and performance data. Depending upon exactly what functions you seek to accomplish in the tutoring center, all of this data might have a valid use. However, legal issues regarding formulation and maintenance of student records need to be carefully considered. While contemplating what records will be maintained, I recommend you first research legal (privacy act) requirements and limitations on establishment, storing, and use of student records. If you believe you need to strengthen your knowledge of privacy issues, I recommend that you talk to guidance personnel in a public school system. They work with these issues on a daily basis and should be very knowledgeable on the subject matter. As part of your thought process regarding need for and establishment of student records, I suggest you address questions such as: why do you need individual student records? What kind of information would be recorded? Do you really need this information? How will the records be secured within the tutoring center? Who will have access to the records? Are you, the parents/guardians, and the students willing to accept that recorded information may possibly be released later as public information? And, perhaps most importantly, how will you ensure that all volunteers follow all requirements of the privacy act?

In consideration of the above factors, I strongly recommend that you start tutoring center operations with very minimal recordkeeping. Perhaps the only student record that should be maintained initially is the sign-in/sign-out log (attachment II-7). The reason for recording this data is primarily to have a record of arrival and departure times in case a need should arise because of some incident involving your students. The attendance data will also be needed if you decide to recognize or reward various levels of student attendance. This approach might sound overly cautious but, again, it is far easier to avoid problems than to resolve difficult issues. Furthermore, it is always possible to establish additional records later if a need becomes apparent.

D. Student Progress

In establishing operating procedures, thought should be given to the issue of student progress. If there is a desire to follow and possibly record student progress, then some form of assessment and evaluation will be needed. This could range from simple tutor comments to feedback from the students' teachers (watch out for the privacy act prohibiting this!) to some form of more formal assessment within the tutoring center. On the other hand, if the goal of your tutoring is simply to assist students with homework and reinforce skills, then much less assessment of student progress would be needed. Either approach can work; you need to clearly define tutoring center goals and plan accordingly. However, I recommend that you initially keep assessment, evaluation, and recording of results to a minimum because these can become challenging and time-consuming tasks that will also add significantly to your training requirements!

E. Emergency Procedures

Emergencies can occur; it's better to be prepared than to be sorry! Following are suggestions for your consideration regarding situations that might arise. This is a sample list and is not meant to be an inclusive list of possible emergencies that you could experience in your tutoring center.

1. Let parents/guardians know what the emergency procedures are for your tutoring center. You might want to have a handout to give to the parents.

2. Consider having a medically qualified person discuss basic emergency considerations during your orientation/ training sessions.

3. Do not attempt to undertake emergency treatments for which you are *not* trained or qualified.

4. Have contact information (names and telephone numbers) readily available for tutoring center staff and ensure that the staff members know where the information is posted.

5. Have a well-supplied medical kit readily available in the tutoring center. I recommend you check with the local Red Cross to help determine the contents of the kit. Be sure the kit includes plastic gloves for staff members to use when treating students.

11. It's Ready to Go, but How Do We Get Started?

As you are completing the many actions necessary to set up your tutoring program, don't forget to include the kickoff event. You need to begin the program with some event that will draw attention to the program within the community and bring parents/guardians to the tutoring center. Remember, in many cases it is the parents/guardians who will be, at least initially, sending the students to you! Depending upon the backgrounds and language limitations of the parents, they may be reluctant to communicate with the tutoring center staff. An icebreaker of some manner is probably needed to begin building a level of trust and confidence. Depending upon the level of involvement of the housing management team, it might be a good idea to send a flyer to all residents informing them that a tutoring (attachment II-3 is one example) program is beginning. Another idea that has worked is to invite parents/guardians to an open house on the first night of tutoring. This gives the parents/guardians a chance to meet the tutoring center staff in a friendly environment, yet also provides an opportunity for parents to register their students (attachment II-3). Another useful icebreaker could be tutors attending community functions for a period of time before the tutoring program commences. For example, if the community has a summer cookout, then why not attend that function, introduce yourself to the neighbors, and hand out flyers (don't forget language problems—think bilingual flyers, etc.). Several ideas might work, but the important goal is to advertise your program, give people a reason to send their students, and demonstrate a friendly, businesslike atmosphere.

12. Daily Tutoring Center Operations

Your tutoring program is about to commence operations. So, just how is your staff going to know what the operational policies and procedures are and what to do as issues arise on a session-by-session basis? One way to address this need is through an operational handbook, which should be immediately available to the staff and updated periodically to ensure relevance.

A. Why a Handbook?

There will be many different people working in many different combinations in the tutoring center. Despite this environment, it is important to ensure continuity in operations from session to session. First, the students will expect a familiar setting in which they can feel safe and comfortable. Second, it is important that the staff has one document for guidance on any subject likely to arise during center operations. Content for the operational handbook will, of course, be determined by the specific needs and structure of your tutoring center program. However, several topics that should be addressed are included in attachment II-1.

B. Environment

Your staff needs to know whether the tutoring center will be operated as a secular or Christian environment. If it is operated as a Christian center, then you must provide guidance on issues such as whether you will open and/or close sessions with prayer; whether tutors will be encouraged to pray with students when appropriate opportunities arise; whether you will invite religious leaders to periodically visit the center; whether you will provide students with Christian literature; and whether you will celebrate Christian holidays in some manner. If you operate the tutoring center on a secular basis, then the tutors need to know what, if any, restrictions are placed on activities within the center.

C. Student and Tutor Expectations

Written guidance should be provided for both students and staff regarding expected and acceptable behavior within the tutoring center. It is important to establish with the students that the assistance being provided is a gift, not a right, and that participation can be terminated for unacceptable behavior. As for staff, it is important to clearly point out what is and is not acceptable adult behavior around young people. This is especially important if some tutors are not familiar with acceptable behavior in an educational environment or perhaps with the legal and moral issues that can arise within academic settings.

D. Receptionist and Supervisor Duties

These are two key positions within the tutoring center, and both have pivotal but different roles to play. The receptionist is the person who keeps the tutoring center functioning smoothly. This person welcomes and signs in the students, determines their support needs, and guides them to the appropriate tutor(s). The receptionist could also be assigned other duties, such as managing the reading library, handling snacks, answering the telephone, and so forth. Having one person assume these functions allows the tutors to focus on tutoring. The supervisor, on the other hand, is the person who is responsible for the overall operation of the center. More specifically, if issues such as student behavior or problems with tutoring center operations occur, the supervisor has the authority to take appropriate action. It is unlikely and frankly unnecessary to have a person identified simply as the supervisor. This is a duty that can easily be assigned to one of the tutors. However, I strongly recommend that a supervisor be identified on the schedule for every tutoring session. In case an incident occurs, it is imperative that the staff knows who is in charge and who is responsible for taking appropriate actions.

E. One-On-One or What?

In an ideal situation, most educators would probably prefer one-on-one tutoring. This approach, of course, requires more tutors, more space, and either a time-sequenced arrival of students or a waiting line in the center. These are issues that should be considered in planning tutoring center operations.

F. Scheduled Times or Open Schedule?

This issue is really part of the topic discussed in the paragraph immediately above. Keep in mind that scheduled times add a function, assumes more responsibility on the part of parents/guardians, and may discourage some students from coming for assistance. On the other hand, scheduled arrivals will avoid an initial rush at the beginning of tutoring sessions and will tend to maintain a calmer atmosphere.

G. Snacks or No Snacks?

Snacks can be a real asset at the center; there is no alternative to a nice snack to "warm up" the atmosphere, especially for the younger students. Also consider that, depending upon times you select for tutoring, students may be coming to you before supper. Keep in mind that while snacks have advantages, they also provide an excuse for lack of focus! I have found that, with proper management, the snacks can be a nice added touch and students rather quickly accept that they are there for tutoring, not for snacks!

13. Attachments

The attachments that follow provide examples of many of the documents that you might choose to use in your tutoring center. Most of these sample documents are referenced in the above paragraphs. These documents, of course, are samples and should be tailored to fit the specific needs of your tutoring center.

I. Topics for Consideration in Planning the Tutoring Center:

1. Considerations for Your Tutoring Center: Frequency and Depth of Assistance

2. Recruitment and Retention of Tutors: Some Considerations

3. Legal and Organizational Issues: Incorporation, Liability Insurance, Board of Directors (or not?)

4. Computer Lab: Issues to Consider

5. Tutoring Center Library: More Issues to Consider!

6. Working with the Supported School System(s): Still More Issues to Mull Over!

7. Checklist for Establishing Your Tutoring Center

8. Sponsoring Organization Support—An Example

II. Examples of Items for Operation of the Tutoring Center

1. Operational Handbook

2. Parent Consent and Expectations Form

3. Sample Flyer

4. Library Sign-In and -Out Form

5. Student Information Form

6. Tutor Schedule Template

7. Student Attendance Log

8. Receptionist Responsibilities

9. Sample—New Volunteer Orientation Session

10. Newsletter Sample

11. Sample List: Tutoring Center Furniture and Supplies

12. Approved Websites

13. Chronological Development of an Onsite Tutoring Program

Attachment I-1

Considerations for Your Tutoring Center: Frequency and Depth of Assistance

Two major factors to consider at the start of planning for your tutoring center is how often will you tutor and to what depth of assistance will you design your center.

Frequency

The question is, basically, what days of the week will you offer tutoring? There are many options. For example, will you tutor every week day, three days a week, two days a week, or just on weekends? Additionally, what time of the day is best for you to operate your center? The answers to these questions will revolve around two issues. First, which option will be best for the students and, second, will you have the resources (tutors as well as other material resources) to tutor as frequently as you might think best? If you have the resources to tutor frequently, you might want to ask whether or not you want to offer tutoring to all grade levels and for all academic subjects at the same time. Keep in mind that, because of peer pressures and tutor background requirements, it might be better to tutor elementary grades, middle school grades, and high school grades on different days or at different times on the same days.

If you find that tutoring less often best meets your neighborhood needs, then the question becomes what days you operate your center. A suggestion regarding this question is to check school schedules. On what days are most tests given? If it's Friday, then perhaps Thursday would be one good day to tutor. What days have the most afterschool events? Perhaps you want to avoid tutoring on this day. Fridays might not be a good day to tutor; after all, who wants to begin the weekend with a tutoring session (that goes for both tutors and students!)? If you tutor two or three days a week, I suggest you not tutor on back-to-back days; spreading the support out over the week will probably be more productive. Again, you need to design your center to meet your neighborhood needs. The above are suggestions meant to help you meet those needs!

Depth of Assistance

By depth of assistance, we mean what level of academic support your tutoring center be designed and equipped to operate.

1. Homework Assistance

Perhaps at the beginning level would be homework support only. This might seem quite limited, but I believe you would be amazed at how much "homework help" your tutors will be providing, how much the students will appreciate this support, and how much difference the assistance can make in the student's performance in school. This first level of support, quite naturally, requires the least amount of support material because the students will bring homework with them to the center. This level will probably also require less academic proficiency on the part of the tutors and will certainly require only limited research materials in the center. It might also be possible to provide this support without online support, meaning no pressing need for a computer lab!

2. Homework and Remedial and Reinforcement (R & R) Support

Adding remedial and reinforcement support brings a major additional commitment on the part of the center and the tutors. To provide good R & R support means the tutoring center must be tied closely to the curriculums of the supported schools. What is not needed for students requiring R & R support is to basically have another curriculum thrown at them in the tutoring center. This factor might be a bit less critical for reinforcement work, but it still makes very good sense to build on what has been presented to students in their school setting rather than striking out to points unknown in the tutoring center! Again, keep in mind that our philosophy is to support the student's regular school process, not to replace it, show it up, or whatever! So, how do you get the needed materials? Good question! This might be one of your more difficult, ongoing challenges in establishing and running your tutoring center.

A. Online Resources

One approach would be to use online resources. However, if you go online, then what resources do you select from the many, many websites that are available? Again, there are many options for this challenge. Please refer to attachment I-4 for more in-depth discussion of the online resources challenge!

B. Hardcopy Resources

Hardcopy resources are available from several sources.

1). You could always purchase materials from the textbook company supporting the local school system. This approach would result in excellent materials that closely parallel the student's daily school work. It would also be a relatively easy route for the tutoring center management to implement. The problem with this approach is cost!

2). Good resources might be available from local schools that your students attend. It is very likely that teachers in the local system have materials or have access to materials that would be excellent for either remedial or reinforcement purposes. Accessing these materials could, however, be a challenge, depending upon the level of mutual support existing between the tutoring center and the local school system.

3). Some good resources might be found on web-based sites or in used bookstores at highly reduced prices from new resources. This approach might take more effort than the above approaches; however, if you like the challenge of bargain hunting, it might be a fun and very rewarding process!

4). In some cases, textbook companies might be willing to provide sample copies of some materials. This is done rather frequently for schools that are in the textbook-selection process. Your ability to get this same support for the tutoring center might be dependent upon your persuasive chatter and good luck! If you decide to give this approach a try, I suggest you start by going through the regional coordinator for the textbook company in question. If that fails, you can still follow up at a higher level in the company hierarchy—good luck!

3. End-of-Year Testing Support

As a result of state and national legislation, essentially all students encounter some form of mandated end-of-year testing. One example of these tests is standards of learning (SOL) tests. You will need to make a decision on whether or not your tutoring center will address support for these mandated tests. On the one hand, material to use for this support is readily available in hardcopy or online resources. The trade off is twofold: first, students probably spend a lot of time during the second half of the spring semester preparing for these tests and, therefore, it may or may not be productive to spend additional time on test preparation in the tutoring center. Second, time spent on these tests will, of course, impact time spent on other tutoring center support.

Attachment I-2

Recruitment and Retention of Tutors: Some Considerations

Wouldn't it be nice if every business had perfect employees who stayed indefinitely and performed every task with perfection? Oh, how easy life could be, if only! But then again, until we are perfect and fit that perfect mold, perhaps we shouldn't expect others to be!

Whatever the cause, I suggest you anticipate a reasonable level of turnover among your volunteers. This, of course, means you should anticipate a reasonable, ongoing challenge of recruiting tutors. So, it makes sense to seek sources of tutors that might meet your needs and, if any, the specific requirements imposed by your sponsoring organization. For example, if you're sponsoring organization specifies that all volunteers be a member of that organization, well then that simplifies and clarifies what your source of tutors will be. Then the challenge will be to convince enough individuals to volunteer to meet your needs; or otherwise, you may have to tailor your level of tutoring support to the available supply of tutors.

But what happens if you are not so tightly restricted in potential sources of tutors? Following are samples of sources you might check out.

1. Sponsoring organization (church, PTA, civic club, police department)
2. Local school systems
3. Companies, especially larger companies that have community support initiatives of various types
4. Retirement communities
5. Retirement associations for professionals

6. Students in area high schools who are seeking service credit hours

7. High school students who are seeking opportunities to serve

8. Other church or civic service organizations beyond your sponsor

9. Consider forming partnerships with community groups to meet mutual needs.

So, if turnover is an issue, what might you do to reduce the significance of the problem? Following are some suggestions for your consideration.

1. Flexibility is the key. Remember, volunteers are busy and are not required to support your project! Be flexible in scheduling, in amount of time required, in number of sessions required per year, in cancellations due to events that arise, etc.

2. Say thank you. It might seem like a little thing, but it's not! People appreciate being told thank you, and letting volunteers know how much their help is appreciated is very important. Tell your volunteers that they are critical to your operation and tell them thank you over and over and over! One neat way to do this is to use little thank you notes, a small token gift (inexpensive being the key!), or perhaps some homebaked cookies—you get the idea!

3. Listen to your tutors. Your tutors will have a fantastic amount of experience in many, many career fields. Together, they have far more cumulative experience than you. Ask for their input and listen—it just may save your center!

4. Keep your volunteers informed. No one likes to be kept in the dark. Let your volunteers know what is going on; too much information is probably better than too little! Try

using bulletin boards, newsletters, and/or periodic (short) meetings. Find what works for you and your environment, but be sure to keep your volunteers informed!

5. Recognize your volunteers. Make it known to your students over and over (and in front of the volunteers) that the adults helping them are volunteering their time and that they are busy people who could very easily spend their time elsewhere. Encourage your students to show respect to the volunteers and to tell them thank you for their help—over and over again!

6. Social events. Yes, our schedules are full. However, try to hold a social event or two for your volunteers each academic year. You might include a short information session with this event, but make it mostly social. It's another way to say thank you and show that you really appreciate volunteer services.

Attachment I-3

Legal and Organizational Issues: Incorporation, Liability Insurance, Board of Directors, etc.

Like it or not, if you set up a tutoring center, there will be issues you must consider beyond tutoring! There will be an ongoing list of issues that will arise. However, three that I believe are especially important are discussed below.

Incorporation

The question is whether you should run your tutoring center as a simple neighborhood outreach ministry/activity and just be happy. This would likely be the preferred method of operation for most of us. However, it might not be the wisest form of organization. Perhaps you should consider some form of incorporation. I am not a lawyer and will not attempt to advise you on this issue other than to suggest that you should be aware of the issue and seek legal advice if you believe such is in your best interest.

Liability Insurance

Whether we like it or not, we must recognize that, just as within other school settings, there is a reasonable chance of a lawsuit arising out of tutor center operations. Remember, anyone in this country can sue, and we have no control over who sues who! The question, then, is how can you best protect yourself against potential lawsuits? One option is, of course, self-insurance. However, for most of us, self-insurance is probably not a reasonable option because of the amounts of money that could be involved. Secondly, we might seek some form of liability insurance. Two sources of this could be your sponsoring organization or your own liability insurance. Again, I am not qualified to offer advice on liability insurance needs or sources. As with incorporation, I only raise the issue for your awareness and suggest you seek appropriate sources of information and advice.

Board of Directors or Steering Committee.

Call it what you choose, but I suggest you need some form of management to assist you with planning, development and operation of your tutoring center. Your specific needs will be influenced by the organizational status of your tutoring center. For example, if you incorporate the tutoring program, your state will define what is needed for a Board and what the composition of the Board must be. On the other hand, if you do not incorporate your tutoring program, you will still want a group of experienced, knowledgeable people to advise you on long range planning, funding and operational issues. You might decide to call this group the Steering Committee. In general, when establishing your Board or Steering Committee, I strongly recommend that you seek people with braod experiences in all aspects of organizational development and operations. It would be especially useful to include members who have previous experience in the world of non-profit organizations. In addition to this executive level body with a long range focus, you will very probably want another body to oversee decisions impacting the short term, almost daily operations of the tutoring program. I will call this body the Tutoring Progrm Management Team.The makeup of this body will largely depend upon your unique circumstances. However, as a general rule, I strongly suggest you try to include a representative from each of the stakeholders in your neighborhood and tutoring center program. For example, you might include representatives from the following:

1. Sponsoring organization
2. Residents from neighborhood being served

3. Rental management or property management office
4. Supported school(s)
5. Volunteers
6. Professional advisers (legal, insurance, etc.)

Attachment I-4

Computer Lab: Issues to Consider

It might seem obvious that you would like to have online access in your tutoring center. However, while it might be obvious that you want access, following are some issues to consider on the way to achieving that access.

1. Sources

From where will you obtain your computers and accessories? Does your program have the financial resources to purchase the computers? If so, good for you! In many cases, you will be seeking donated resources. I suggest you be creative in the sources you seek out, as there are many programs out there. For example, some churches have computer donation programs; many telecommunication companies offer programs to donate used machines; many large (and some not-so-large) companies update computers rather frequently and may be more than happy to donate some of their old computers and accessories to your program; grants just might be available to acquire computers (and other support as well) for your center; and some school systems have specific sites to which people can turn to request donation of "old" computers. This sampling is intended to whet your appetite! Be confident that you can find computers—just go for it!

2. Wi-Fi or Not?

The decision regarding hardwired connectivity vs. wireless connectivity will largely be driven by connectivity options available in the space obtained for your tutoring center. The good news is that either wi-fi or cable will meet your needs. The more difficult challenge might be talking the donor of your spaces into providing internet access if it is not already available in the building. In this case, you might check with your local internet provider(s) to see if there is a possibility of a line being donated for your use. Overall, we suggest that internet access be one of the "requirements" you state when initially seeking space for your tutoring center.

3. How Many Stations?

This is a good question. Ideally, it might be nice to have a computer for each student on each shift. However, this often may not be practical. What we have found is that it works quite well to rotate students through "stations" (homework, remedial work, reinforcement work, bonus time). This approach significantly reduces the number of computers your center needs (versus wants!) to still address the needs of all the students.

Attachment I-5

Tutoring Center Library:
More Issues to Consider!

Should you build a library, why and what would you include in your library? These, perhaps, are the questions you might be asking! Well, the reason for having a library is partially driven by the level of academic support your tutoring center is designed to provide. Observations, with suggestions, follow.

Reading Library

Perhaps the most basic library would be a reading library, primarily for elementary grade students. The purpose for such a library is, essentially, threefold: first, encourage students to read by encouraging them to sign books out to read at home. Second, students will often have reading homework assignments but may often neglect to bring a book with them to the tutoring session. Often times, the reading assignment might be to read for some period of time and have that reading documented in a reading log. Having a reading library within the tutoring center can certainly facilitate this process! A third reason for having a reading library is, perhaps, more related to mentoring than to tutoring! Students who attend tutoring from the neighborhoods we work with are often seeking reassurance or approval. These students often stay around the tutoring center beyond the time it takes just to complete their homework, etc. In many cases, curling up with a book in the tutoring center might be just what the doctor ordered!

Remedial and Reinforcement Support

As you increase the level of academic support promised, it's imperative that you provide adequate research materials for both students and tutors. As a minimum, it is very helpful, almost essential, that you have student or teacher editions of textbooks students are using in their regular schools. In addition, it can be very helpful to have a few well-selected reference books in a variety of fields (math, science, language, poetry, etc.) at student and teacher fingertips in your center. And, of course, don't over look your internet access; online sites are a fantastic reference source when you can't quite recall that specific item you had in class fifteen (or was it twenty!) years ago. Students also like the opportunity to research topics online. Remember, many of the students coming to your tutoring center may not have online access in their homes. You might be surprised how often our students have a project for homework that requires internet access; we attempt to provide this access in every tutoring center the NTP operates.

Sources

So, if you decide to establish a library, from where are you going to get books or other resources? Well, fortunately there are lots of good books lying around in people's unused spaces! Asking for book donations can yield a rich, free return! Secondly, there are many sources for very inexpensive used books; search these out in your neighborhood and make use of the materials you find! Then, if all else fails, have some fun and go around to used book stores and find some super values; you really can find bunches of books for very reasonable cost! And, of course, don't overlook the used book websites on the good old internet. While shipping costs can be a problem, the cost of the books can be very, very reasonable!

And don't overlook the internet! Assuming you have internet access in your tutoring center, there are many online websites that offer excellent reading and research resources and often with fun twists thrown into the mix—guess it's time to do some Google searches! And, by the way, why not let that student who is always offering to help do some searching? He or she just might be much more proficient on the internet than you are!

Also, don't overlook your local school's teachers' websites. They often contain online resources that are suggested sites for parents and students to access in the home environment. These same teacher sites can be a good source of sites for you, especially if you feel your knowledge of potentially useful sites is limited.

And finally, be creative! For example, in some of our NTP-operated tutoring centers, we have had the luxury of support from professionally trained reading dogs. There are several organizations that offer this service, and most elementary students are enthusiastic to "read to the dog." And for you doubters, research indicates that many students who consider themselves to be poor readers prefer to "read to the dog" instead of to humans because the dogs are far less critical! Check it out! (Refer to attachment II-12 for a sampling of useful websites.)

Attachment I-6

Working with Supported School Systems: Still More Issues to Mull Over!

We have stressed throughout this document that the philosophy of the NTP is to support the educational process and school in which the students are regularly enrolled. This approach might seem logical and simple. Logical, perhaps so; simple, not so fast!

Most school systems will probably be very supportive of the mission of your tutoring center. In fact, most school systems will probably state that they are willing to support you in any way they can. But therein lays the rub: *in any way they can.* Most school systems, especially public school systems, are very restricted in what information they can share or provide to whom. Violating these laws could and likely would result in more legal issues than you or the school system would prefer to handle! Therefore, it is important to be realistic when developing working relationships with supported schools. I strongly suggest you approach a school from the top; introduce yourself to school administrators and to the head of the guidance department before attempting to work directly with teachers. This approach recognizes and shows respect to the structure of the school and will most probably pay dividends down the road. It would also be a good idea to introduce yourself to whatever parent-teacher association (PTA, etc.) is functioning in the school of interest. This organization deserves to know what you are planning and can potentially be one of your best sources of moral support (and perhaps other forms).

Working directly with teachers could be very useful. However, again, the teachers are very restricted in what they can provide you in terms of student performance or needs. Teachers might better be looked to as potential sources of support for remedial or reinforcement materials. In addition, don't count out the teacher websites as a good source of sites for parent-student use. These sites might be a good starting point for some of your online support.

And, as a minimum, be sure the supported schools know your tutoring centers exist! As a minimum, the guidance department can certainly have information on where your site is located and the forms of support you provide. Students often check with their guidance counselors for sources of tutors, and it is certainly to your advantage if you are known by these counselors.

And finally, don't count out residents of your neighborhood who are employees of the supported schools. If willing, these individuals can be a good source of information from you into the schools. Just as valuable, these individuals can be an excellent source of general information for you; they may be good people to include on your Tutoring Program Management Team(Refer to Attachment I-3). Remember, relationships are everything, and effective two-way communication is certainly a critical part of that relationship!

Attachment I-7

Tutoring Center Startup Checklist

	Action Item	Priority	Person (s)	Due Date
1	Identify sponsoring organization	1		
2	Identify facility	1		
3	Ensure facility availability	1		
4	ID tutoring source(s)	1		
5	ID funding needs	1		
6	Develop partnerships as needed	1		
7	Plan recruitment program	2		
8	Acquire remedial/ reinforcement material	2		
9	Determine who will conduct background investigations; cost?	2		
10	Plan/set up reading library	2		
11	Acquire center furniture ★	2		
12	Coordinate with police, etc.	2		
13	Coordinate with supported schools	2		
14	Plan for computer acquisition	2		
15	Plan security program (physical, document)	2		
16	Plan for internet access	2		
17	Acquire books & materials	2		

18	Identify online resources to use	2		
19	Acquire needed codes, etc. for online sites	3		
20	Recruit tutors and receptionists	3		
21	Tutor orientation	3		
22	Plan and write operational handbook	3		
23	Conduct background investigations	3		
24	Identify funding needs	3		
25	Plan program startup publicity	3		
26	Develop tutor schedule	3		
27	Plan, conduct startup publicity	3		
28	Identify shift supervisor	3		
29	Acquire basic school supplies ★★★★	3		
30	Arrange publicity for opening session	3		
31	Acquire misc. items for the center★★	4		
32	Send out flyers to client homes	4		
33	Plan opening session	4		
34	Copy all forms★★★	4		
35	Set up center tables, etc.	4		
36	Acquire emergency phone #s at student sign in	4		
37	Verify staff is ready to start	4		
38	Arrange for snacks, utensils	4		

★	Book case(s), tables/desks, lights, wall hangings, receptionist desk			
★★	Toilet paper, etc., rubber gloves			
★★★	Parent consent, flyers, sign-in/sign-out forms, tutor schedules			
★★★★	pencils, scissors, glue sticks, scratch paper, lined paper, color pencils, crayons, rulers (metric and US), pencil sharpener, timers, paper clips, alligator clips, etc.			

Attachment I-8

Sponsoring Organization Support—An Example

The Neighborhood Tutoring Program is, by design, a volunteer-based program. Therefore, when using the NTP model to develop your tutoring center, it's imperative that you look for sources of support where available. This appendix provides an example of how one sponsoring organization and other community resources supported development and operation of it's center. In this case, the sponsor was a church; the examples are actual events for this particular center. Similar types of support could also be arranged with other nonchurch, civic-oriented sponsors.

Funding

A tutoring center can be developed and operated with very reasonable funding. The main setup costs are for basic furniture (tables, chairs, bookcase, etc.) and school supplies. Many of these items can be obtained through donations or purchased from discount sources such as Salvation Army, consignment businesses, and so forth. Practically speaking, there are two likely funding sources; one or a few individuals that choose to fund the project or donated funds from members of the sponsoring organization. In this respect, churches are good sponsoring organizations because they probably have an existing process through which funds can be sought and managed through a tax-exempt process. In our example, an account was set up within the church budget for the tutoring center. Donated funds were then earmarked for the center, which provided tax deductions for the donors. Also keep in mind that some churches might decide to include tutoring center support as a line item in the annual budget.

Staffing

The most obvious source of staffing will probably be the sponsoring organization. One approach would be for some group within the church to take on staffing as a ministry. Otherwise, requests for tutors can be easily made through the existing announcement process or bulletin used in the church. There are also other potential sources for tutors, including staff members from neighborhood schools, other area churches, area retirement communities, organizations of retired professionals, community businesses, and civic associations. In our example, staffing needs were met through the sponsoring church.

Tax Status

I would advise getting tax exempt (IRS 501 C-3, etc.) status for your center. The major benefit is simple; it is financially attractive for individuals to make cash or other kinds of donations to tax-exempt organizations. An advantage of being sponsored by a church is that the tax-exempt status is more than likely already established. If you choose to arrange tax-exempt status specifically for your center, then the application process is readily available from the Internal Revenue Service.

Materials

You will need an assortment of educational materials to operate your center. Some of these materials, such as textbooks, worksheets etc., are obvious. One need that may test your ingenuity is material for the character-building phase of your sessions. In many cases, your sponsoring organization may be the best source for these materials. For instance, in our example, materials used in the church's elementary and young adult programs have been donated to the tutoring center. These materials have often formed the nucleus around which a short activity was based, and these materials are often sent home with the students. Nonchurch, civic-oriented sponsors might also have materials for use in a similar fashion.

Speakers and Other Extra Events

We all like to have fun, and learning should be fun! In addition, we have found that attendance at our tutoring centers has been very consistent. Therefore, a good measure of mentoring actually occurs within the tutoring center. As a result, students often develop a real attachment to the tutoring center and to the volunteers working in the center. Take advantage of these opportunities; make the center fun! If your center is church sponsored, you might want to have fun little parties on special church holidays. The same could be done with other civic-oriented sponsors by simply changing the holidays! Perhaps you want to recognize birthdays. We all like to be recognized on our special day, and it can be done at very reasonable cost! Special recognition students have earned at school (honor role, science fair recognition, music awards, etc.) can be acknowledged. The list is endless, and we have found that the students are more than willing to share their good news with you, so it's easy to gather the data!

How about bringing in fresh faces to share with the students on some interesting topic? If church sponsored, bring in a minister or other church official; how about bringing in someone who has been recognized within the community for their volunteer work? Again, the list of possibilities is endless. Remember, the purpose for these activities is to address students' self-esteem and confidence. Never under estimate the impact these activities might have on your students. And, keep in mind that improved self-esteem and confidence may well be two of your students' greatest needs!

Attachment II-1

Operational Handbook

An operational handbook should be developed for each tutoring center and should be maintained in a current status. The handbook should be kept in a place that is known to all staff members. In addition, the staff members should be made clearly aware that they are expected to know and follow the procedures established in the handbook. Handbook content and location are topics that you might want to include in new volunteer orientation sessions.

Content for the operational handbook should be tailored to the needs of your particular tutoring center and staff. For your reference, following is a list of topics included in the operational handbook for one of the tutoring centers operated by the NTP:

I.   Tutor Center Operating Procedures

II.   Tutors—Guidelines

III. Expectations: Students, Parents/Guardians, Staff, and Supervisor.

IV.   Receptionist Responsibilities

V.   Parent(s)/Guardian(s) Consent and Expectation Form

VI.   Student Attendance Log

VII. Tutor Schedule

VIII. Approved Websites

IX.   Parking Procedures and Passes

If desired, a complete copy of this operational handbook can be provided to you. Contact the NTP offices at the following e-mail address to request an electronic copy of the handbook. There is no charge for this copy.

E-mail Address: Dmiller832@comcast.net

Attachment II-2

Parent Consent and Expectation Form

Parent(s)/Guardian(s) Consent Form: Neighborhood Tutoring Program

I (We) have read and understand the terms in the Expectation Form (on page two of this form) for the tutoring center. We concur with the expectations for parents/guardians and for students and will ensure that our student follows established rules and procedures. We further understand that if our student fails to follow the student expectations, he or she may be banned from the tutoring center. We also understand that it is our responsibility to transport our student to and from the tutoring center and that the tutoring center is responsible for our student only during the time our student is actually in the tutoring center for academic assistance. We acknowledge and concur with the tutorial assistance being provided through the tutoring program.

Parent/Guardian Name: (Print) _____

Parent/Guardian Signature: _____

Student(s) Name: (Print) _____

Telephone Number at Which Parent Can Be Reached During Tutoring: _____

Forma del consentimiento de los padres/de los guardas: Programa del curso particular de la vecindad

I (Nosotros) ha leído y entiende los términos en la forma de la expectativa (en revés de esta forma) para el centro del curso particular. Concurrimos con las expectativas para los padres/los guardas y para los estudiantes y nos aseguraremos de que nuestro estudiante sigue reglas y procedimientos establecidos. Entendemos más lejos que si nuestro estudiante no puede seguir las expectativas he or she del estudiante se pueden prohibir del centro del curso particular. También entendemos que es nuestra responsabilidad transportar a nuestro estudiante a y desde el centro del curso particular y que el centro del curso particular es responsable de nuestro estudiante solamente durante el tiempo nuestro estudiante está realmente en el centro del curso particular para la ayuda académica. Reconocemos y concurrimos con la ayuda que es proporcionada con el programa del curso particular.

Nombre del padre/del guarda: _____ (de la impresión)
Firma del padre/del guarda:_____
Nombre de los estudiantes: _____ (de la impresión)
Número de teléfono en el cual el padre puede ser
alcanzado durante curso particular: _____

Student and Parent Expectations

Student expectations:

1. Come properly attired; see the section on dress.
2. Proper behavior is to be displayed at all times.
3. Proper respect is to be shown at all times to tutor center staff and to other students.
4. Come to the center with specific questions or areas of need in mind.
5. Bring textbooks (or handouts) and homework with you for those subjects in which you need assistance.
6. Bring whatever tools (e.g., ruler, calculator, and protractor) are necessary to enable the tutor to provide the desired assistance.
7. Improper dress, behavior, preparation, or lack of effort will be reason for a student to be dismissed from the tutor center; repeated violations in these areas could result in long-term or permanent banning from the tutoring center.

Parents/Guardians: Learning is a multifaceted process that involves teamwork. Student, tutor, parents, and supervisors all have a critical role to play to make this program successful for each individual student. With this in mind, parents/guardians are to do the following:

1. Accompany their student to the center for the initial visit to meet the staff and to ensure they understand the processes used in the tutoring center
2. Read this expectation sheet and ask any questions they might have regarding its contents
3. Read and sign the consent form authorizing their student to participate in the tutoring center program
4. Take responsibility to ensure that their student(s) are safely brought to the tutoring center and picked up for the return trip to the student's home
5. Acknowledge, by signing the consent form, that the tutoring center is not responsible for safety of students outside of the immediate confines of the tutoring center
6. Immediately inform tutoring center staff of any concerns or issues that they, the parents/guardians, might have regarding any facet of tutoring center operations

(See reverse of this form for Spanish version of the statement.)

Expectativas del estudiante y del padre

Expectativas del estudiante:

1. Venido correctamente attired; vea la sección en el vestido.
2. El comportamiento apropiado debe ser exhibido siempre.
3. El respeto apropiado debe ser demostrado en todas las veces al personal del centro del profesor particular y a otros estudiantes.

4. Venido al centro con preguntas o áreas específicas de la necesidad en mente.

5. Traiga los libros de textos (o los folletos) y la preparación con usted para esos temas adentro cuál usted necesita ayuda.

6. Traiga cualesquiera herramientas (e.g., la regla, la calculadora, y el prolongador) son necesarios permitir al profesor particular proporcionar la ayuda deseada.

7. El vestido incorrecto, el comportamiento, la preparación o la carencia del esfuerzo serán razón para que un estudiante sea despedido del centro del profesor particular; las violaciones repetidas en estas áreas podían dar lugar a la prohibición a largo plazo o permanente del centro del curso particular.

Padres/guardas: El aprender es un proceso multifaceted que implica trabajo en equipo. El estudiante, el profesor particular, los padres y los supervisores todo tienen un papel crítico a jugar para hacer este programa acertado para cada estudiante individual. Con esto en mente, los padres/los guardas están:

1. Acompañe a su estudiante al centro para que la visita inicial satisfaga a personal y asegurar lo entiende los procesos usados en el centro del curso particular

2. Lea esta hoja de la expectativa y haga cualquier pregunta que ella puede ser que tenga con respecto a su contenido

3. Leído y firme la forma del consentimiento que autoriza a su estudiante a participar en el programa del centro del curso particular

4. Tome la responsabilidad de asegurarse de que traen al centro del curso particular y están tomados sus estudiantes con seguridad para el viaje de vuelta al hogar del estudiante

5. Reconozca, firmando la forma del consentimiento, que el centro del curso particular no es responsable de la seguridad de estudiantes fuera de los límites inmediatos del centro del curso particular

6. Informe inmediatamente al personal de centro del curso particular cualesquiera preocupaciones o edición que, el padre/guarda, puede ser que tengan con respecto a cualquier faceta de las operaciones del centro del curso particular

Attachment II-3

Sample Flyer

Free Tutoring for
Coverstone IV Residents – Grades K-12
All Academic Subjects

(excludes foreign languages and specialty areas such as music, PE, tech courses, and advanced courses like AP, college credit, etc.)

Location: (in the Coverstone IV neighborhood) Prince William County Police – Coverstone IV Field Station 7654 Cass Place

Tuesday and Thursday Evenings
5:30 pm – 7:30 pm

This program was started this fall semester. It is guided by a certified teacher (K-12, math & social studies) with over twenty years of teaching experience. We have approximately twenty-five volunteer tutors, the majority of whom are either current or retired teachers. The response has been outstanding, with fifteen to twenty-five students coming for tutoring each session. We are very serious about aligning our efforts with those of the three schools the students attend (Mullen ES; Marsteller MS; Stonewall Jackson HS).

For information, contact Mr. Duane Miller, tel: 703-743-1974

E-mail: dmiller832@comcast.net

Open House

WHEN: Tuesday Oct 5th, 5:30 – 7:30 pm

Thursday Oct 7th, 5:30 – 7:30 pm

WHERE: Coverstone IV Community Room
(Light refreshments served)

WHY: •   Get information about the free tutoring
program being offered in Coverstone IV

•   Parents can sign their student(s) up for
the tutoring program

•   Opportunity to meet the tutors

•   Ask any questions you have about the
program

•   Get your questions answered

Hope to see you at the Open House!

Attachment II-4

Library Sign-In and Sign-Out Form

NAME	BOOK	DATE OUT	DATE RETURNED

Attachment II-5

Student Information Form

Student's Name	
School	
Grade and Age	
Siblings Names and Ages	
Date and Tutor's Name	
During today's session we worked on:	
Date and Tutor's Name	
During today's session we worked on:	
Date and Tutor's Name	
During today's session we worked on:	
Date and Tutor's Name	
During today's session we worked on:	
Date and Tutor's Name	
During today's session we worked on:	
Date and Tutor's Name	
During today's session we worked on:	

Attachment II-6

Tutor Schedule Template

Tutoring Center Schedule 12 January 2011						
Date	Receptionist	Math	Elementary	Reading	General	# Staff
NOTE: In actuality, this form is in Excell format and updated as needed throughout semester						

Note: This matrix is meant to be used for scheduling tutors. It is not meant to be used for scheduling students for assistance in the tutoring center. Names of tutors are entered into the boxes on the schedule for each tutoring session.

Attachment II-7

Student Attendance Log

	A	B	C	D	E
1			Tutor Log		
2	DATE	STUDENT NAME	IN	OUT	TUTOR
3					
4					
5					
6					
7					

NOTE: This form is maintained as an Excel spreadsheet, with copies run off as needed.

Attachment II-8

Receptionist Responsibilities

Set up the receptionist desk near the front door. The following items are needed at the receptionist desk:

- Tutor schedule
- Student sign-in/sign-out log
- Parking pass log (if parking passes are issued)
- Parking passes (volunteers)
- Volunteer name tags
- Student name tags
- "Goodie bag"
- Snacks for tables
- Library sign-in/sign-out book

Receptionist Duties (sample):

1. Provide a parking pass to each volunteer; log the pass number on the parking pass log.

2. Sign all students in on the student log; assign them to a tutor and give them a name tag (if used).

3. Have students wait on couch if there is no available tutor.

4. Monitor activity on porch; Note: it is *not* your responsibility to tell kids/adults to leave the porch. However, if you see people congregating there, please inform the tutoring center supervisor.

5. Sign students out as they depart; inform them that they are not to return after completing work and departing.

6. Do not allow students to remain in the tutoring center if they did *not* come for tutoring (e.g., came along with a friend).

7. Give students a treat from the goodie bag (healthy snacks or occasionally candy!) as they depart.

8. Remind students that they are *not* to return once they depart.

9. Collect parking passes from volunteers as they depart; log return of passes into the parking pass log.

10. Manage the library book sign-in and sign-out process.

Set up and manage distribution of the snacks.

Attachment II-9

Sample—New Volunteer Orientation Session

Neighborhood Tutoring Ministry
Information Meeting
Aug 14, 21 2011

1. Welcome

2. Introductions

3. Background and Status—NTP

   - Had a successful first year—AY 2010-2011
   - Fits in nicely as one part of the broader Coverstone IV Outreach Ministry
   - Tutor from 5:30–7:30 Tuesdays and Thursdays
   - All volunteer program—flexible schedules and commitments
   - Great support from Coverstone IV management
   - Plan to expand to a second center near Coverstone IV
     - Working on this project
     - May start on a very small scale
   - Background Investigations
     - Background investigations are required for all volunteers and employees.
     - Pass out sheets, fill in, and return to me and I'll get them turned in

4. Concept of operations—highlight some items of special importance to me!

- Mission—Represent Christ in the Coverstone IV neighborhood; tutoring is a tool to work through to accomplish this objective.
- Goal: cover several subjects and grades (lower elementary through middle school/high school)
  - First help with homework, then remediate/reinforce
  - Emphasis on mathematics and language arts
  - Introducing use of computers for remediation
  - Working to supplement PWCS program vs. a separate curriculum
- Operate during fall and spring semester (no summer school)
- start a bit after school starts in fall and spring
  - Tutoring begins 9/20/2011
  - take time off over Christmas (fall tutoring will end 12/6)
- Independent of public schools but keep in contact with guidance counselors
  - We want to be a known referral source in the schools
  - Mullen Elementary, Marstellar MS, Stonewall Jackson HS
- Be a first-class operation
  - Expect great things;
  - Do not accept less than the best we can give and the children can deliver.
- Materials: we will provide paper, pencils, etc; will try to get copies of most commonly used textbooks.

5. Volunteer Positions

- Receptionist
- Tutors
  - Educational background not needed
  - Prior tutoring experience not needed

- High school seniors (honor students, etc.) through adults
- Background Investigations
    - Background investigations are required for all volunteers and employees
- Pass out sheets, fill in, and return to me and I'll get them turned in
- Schedules: how often must you work?
    - Flexible schedules
    - No specific requirements
    - Would like one-year commitment

6. Orientation Sessions for new tutors

- Tuesdays, August 23, 30; Sept 6, 13.
- Onsite

7. Questions?

Attachment II-10

Newsletter Sample

Neighborhood Tutoring Program (NTP)
Newsletter
Dec 14, 2010

The purpose of this newsletter is to bring all NTP volunteers to a common point with regard to program status, developments and upcoming initiatives. In the future, newsletters will be sent out at least once a semester to keep everyone informed. Please direct any questions, suggestions, or recommendations to Duane Miller, tel: 703-743-1974 or e-mail: dmiller832@comcast.net.

I. Fall Semester 2010-2011

1. Current Operations: We completed the fall semester on Dec. 9 with our special Christmas Party session. Overall attendance this fall was great. We built up to a level of 25 or 26 students on three sessions, then dropped to around 12–15 once daylight savings time ended and it got colder. The 12–15 students are almost totally repeats, who tell us they really look forward to coming to tutoring. We have found 12–15 students work very well within our limited spaces. It gives each tutor 2–3 students, which is very conducive to individual assistance. Most students come at 5:30 and almost all have arrived at 6:00 p.m. Most of the tutoring assistance begins to wrap up around 7:00 p.m. We have been starting each session with a brief "children's story" and prayer. The students have reacted very positively to this Christ-centered orientation.

2. Operating Procedures Handbook Update: A review and update of NTP operating procedures will be conducted during the remainder of December. Mr. Miller will send an e-mail to all volunteers asking for input, will then update the procedures handbook, and submit it to volunteers for use during the spring semester. Several incidents (positive ones!) occurred during the fall semester, confirming the need to maintain an up-to-date set of operating procedures.

3. Kid's Quest Materials: Kid's Quest has been providing us materials from their Sunday programs. We are using these materials as handouts to send home with the NTP students. We are in the process of refining which Kid's Quest materials are most practical for NTP use.

4. PWCS Support: The Prince William County School System (PWCS) has been most cooperative in supporting the NTP mission. Duane Miller is working with representatives from Mullen ES, Marsteller MS, Stonewall Jackson HS, and the PWCS mathematics department. He has been invited to attend elementary school training sessions on their math curriculum, and the PWCS has provided NTP with a set of elementary materials for grades one through five. Also, working through the Marsteller MS guidance department, Duane is in the process of establishing working relationships with each grade team. As a part of this process, one of the local textbook representatives has agreed to provide NTP a set of teachers-edition textbooks and student workbooks for both course 2 and course 3 (seventh and eighth grades).These materials are expected to be available for the spring semester.

5. Reading Program: Establishment of a reading library to support the reading program is well underway. Ms. Jones, and Ms. Peterson have donated a large number of books appropriate for our elementary and middle school students. Ms. Johnson plans to review these materials and rate them for grade level.

6. Math Program: Duane is in the process of integrating materials provided by the PWCS system into a filing/access system that supports our NTP operating concept. The goal will be, by beginning of the spring semester, to have NTP materials arranged in an easily accessible manner that aligns with the sequence (pacing) followed by PWCS.

7. Donor Program: Janice Goodman has taken the lead to plan a donor program for the NTP. This program, initially viewed as a source of obtaining textbooks, may be broadened to also address other material needs.

8. High School Student Involvement: To date, we have been unsuccessful at attracting Coverstone IV high school students to the tutoring center. Several attempts have been made to reach out to this group of students. Please keep this portion of our ministry in your prayers.

9. Core Team: Our sponsor requires the NTP to have a Core Team. The Core Team is basically a steering committee.

The NTP Core Team meets as needs dictate. All NTP volunteers are welcome and encouraged to attend the core team meetings. As the agenda is set for each meeting, an e-mail will be sent to all volunteers informing them of the meeting, inviting them to attend and welcoming inputs to the agenda for the upcoming meeting.

II. Spring Semester

1. Dates: Spring semester tutoring dates will be coordinated with volunteers via e-mail over the next two weeks. Tentatively, we are thinking of beginning tutoring on Thursday, January 14 with an open house, just as we did at the beginning of the fall semester. This worked well in the fall and would provide an opportunity to attract new families for the spring.

2. Inclement Weather: The NTP will follow PWCS decisions on weather-related closings. If PWCS schools are closed for a day, we will not have tutoring that evening.

3. Volunteer Schedule: The volunteer spring schedule will be worked via e-mail during the next three weeks. We will use a process similar to that used for scheduling during the fall semester.

4. SOL Preparation: As with most school systems, SOL Preparation receives a great deal of attention during the second half of the spring semester. Based on discussions with PWCS personnel, I believe we could best assist our students during the late spring by placing emphasis on the SOL topics; Virginia State and other SOL materials are readily available on the internet. More information will be provided on this topic as spring approaches.

III. New Initiatives.

As we look forward, there are several initiatives to be worked, including the following:

1. Computers in Tutoring Center: Computer-assisted learning can be very valuable for some students. Duane is pursuing acquisition of one or two computers for the NTP. In addition to instructional materials, the computers would be useful for administrative functions within the NTP.

2. Automated Scheduling: Methods other than Excel via e-mail will be explored for schedule maintenance. Google Calendar might be one possibility. Other suggestions are welcome.

IV. Second Tutoring Site—Explore.

One of the goals of the NTP program is to develop a model Neighborhood Tutoring Program that can be easily exported to other communities. Duane, with core team guidance, will continue to work on this facet of the NTP. Any suggestions are welcome.

V. Prayer.

The NTP is the Lord's program. This program will succeed with His support and guidance. On the other hand, the program will likely never attain its full potential without the support and guidance of the Lord. Please pray for His continuing guidance and blessing.

Attachment II-11

Sample List: Tutoring Center Furniture and Supplies

This is a sample list of furniture and supply items necessary to operate the NTP tutoring center. The list is not meant to be exhaustive and will need to be adjusted to fit the needs of each specific center.

a. Furniture: tables and chairs for tutoring

b. Bookcase

c. Academic materials (including character building and self-image)

d. Snacks

e. Eating utensils

f. Filing cabinet

g. Sign-in/-out book

h. County school system books/curriculum/pacing guides

i. Bathroom facility and supplies

j. Telephone and emergency contact numbers

k. Rubber gloves (supplies) for cleaning up messes

l. Receptionist "desk"

m. Basic school supplies (pencils, pens, colored pencils, scrap paper, stapler, scissors, clips, pencil sharpener, wall posters)

n. Decorative wall hangings

o. Computers and accessories (if computer use is planned)

Attachment II-12

Approved Websites

I strongly recommend that you maintain a list of approved websites for students to access while working on computers in your tutoring center. The sites on your approved list will vary depending upon the goals of your center. I also recommend that you do not include social sites on the approved list. The list that follows is simply a starting point. The list is somewhat math oriented and, in any case, needs to be periodically updated since websites come and go!

http://pwcs.edu (Go to your class, room, etc.) This is a county school system site. Each school your tutoring center program supports will probably have a similar site.

http://www.starfall.com

http://www.poptropica.com

http://www.coolmath.com

http://www:funbrain.com

http://brainpopjr.com

http://spellingcity.com

http://www.jumpstart.com/free-online-game.aspx?pid=display&cid=728&qclid=COrPqbHBxqsCFQtb7Aodm36k7A

http://www.playkidsgames.com/

http://www.raz-kids.com/

http://solpass.org

http://www.wendyseqer.com (SOL Review Games)

http://funschool.kaboose.com/index.html

http://sheppardsoftware.com/mathgames/fruitshoot/fruitshoot.addition.html

http://www.sachem.edu/dept/sd/smarboard/Elementary%20Resources.htm

http://www.abcya.com

http://www.playkidsgames.com/

http://www.jumpstart.com

http://www.wacona.com/kindergartengames

http://www.multiplication.com

http://www.arcademicskillbuilders.com

http://www.studyisland.com

http://mathproblems.info

http://mathforum.org/dr.math/

http://www.tumblebooks

http://www.excelleratedreader

http://www.mff.org/mmc/muskrat_math_game.pdf

http://Discoverykids.com

http://mathfactcafe.com/

http://education.jlab.org/solquiz/index.html

http://math_mania/math.html

http://.cobbk12.org/sites/literacy/math/math2.

www.math.com

www.mathgooodies.com

www.sosmath.com

www.webmath.com

www.algebrahelp.com

www.scilinks.org

Consider looking at the textbooks used in the supported school. Most of the textbooks will include websites that can be accessed for free and have wonderful materials.

Attachment II-13

Chronological Development of an Onsite Tutoring Program

Attachment I-7 provides a good checklist to help steer planning and development of your tutoring center. However, in discussions with friends and advisors while writing this book, it has been suggested that a chronological list of steps, or perhaps phase points, would be useful. This attachment provides that tool. However, keep in mind that the exact order of events will surely change from program to program. For each step listed below, there is a section in the book titled *The Neighborhood Tutoring Program* that addresses the topic in detail. These are cross-referenced in the paragraphs below.

1. If your organization is sensing a desire to undertake a ministry, pray, discuss, and educate yourselves regarding the range of opportunities available and the benefits and costs of each.

2. Determine, through lengthy analysis, that your organization will sponsor an onsite tutoring center.

3-4. Select a target community for the onsite tutoring center program. Use a clearly established set of criteria for evaluating various communities. Be able to clearly explain why the particular community was selected over other candidates.

3-4. Hold meetings with the power structure(s) involved to determine whether or not you can win their support behind the proposed tutoring center program. Following are some potential power centers: owner/property management for the site; community leaders within the targeted community; other community civic or religious organizations already serving in the community (e.g., is there a need for the service you are proposing and will your program be welcomed or shunned by the current players?); security personnel (what kind of neighborhood are you about to move into?); school leaders (is there a need for tutoring within the community and can you expect an adequate level of support from the school system?); community civic and business leaders.

5. Identify a potential site for the tutoring center within the selected community.

6. Begin planning and development for the actual program. Your organization is now the sponsoring organization.

A. Establish a management structure for guiding the onsite tutoring project. Include a prayer team within this structure.

B. Determine whether your sponsoring organization can and will be provide liability insurance and whether you will choose to incorporate your tutoring center program. Take additional actions needed depending upon the answers to these questions.

C. Identify your funding source(s) for the development and operation of your tutoring center; confirm that financial source is firm.

D. Define the mission, level of support, days of operation, hours of operation, etc. for your center. Don't forget to consider snacks, libraries, and so forth. Use this process to initially identify the approximate number of tutors you will need.

E. Define whether or not you will include a computer lab in the tutoring center; if so, begin to plan for acquisition of the computers, internet access, financial needs, etc.

F. Identify the source(s) for recruiting tutors; discuss the potential for recruiting adequate numbers of tutors and the processes to be followed in the recruiting program. If needed, identify additional sources for tutors. Start developing partnerships if the need is identified to get adequate numbers of tutors.

G. Begin to advertise your tutoring program within the target community; attend community events, send out flyers, etc.

H. Become very familiar with the curriculums and structures in the school systems your program will support. Identify which books and other educational materials you would like to acquire for your center. Look for acquisition opportunities for these materials. As part of this process, determine whether or not there are software programs in the school systems that you would like to have your students access in your tutoring centers. If there are, talk to the IT department in the schools and determine if you will be allowed to access the data programs and what access codes will be needed.

I. Begin to identify on-site websites that you will use; plan the actual educational methodology that will be employed in the center (e.g., one-on-one tutoring, team tutoring, education stations, etc.).

J. Identify other sources for the educational materials you will need and pursue those sources. Begin to acquire basic center supplies: furniture, school supplies, etc.

K. Begin to think seriously about and perhaps start your tutor recruitment program. Don't forget to recruit receptionists.

L. Identify what security procedures will be needed at your center (personal security in parking lots, student record security, etc.) Identify who you need to talk to determine your needs and to establish the needed security. Identify names and telephone numbers of security personnel.

M. Develop an operational handbook for the tutoring center.

N. Be sure your tutor recruiting program is yielding results and plan accordingly; include tutor orientation and training as part of this program.

O. Set up and check out your computer lab. Complete and post operating procedures, etc.

P. Plan for a kickoff event. Invite opening day dignitaries, etc.

Q. Develop and publish a tutor schedule; do this on a semester basis with monthly or weekly updates. Send out weekly reminders (e-mail, texting, or whatever media you choose).

R. Get door-to-door start out publicity campaign underway (this should be a week or so before start up).

S. Acquire snacks, etc.

T. Last minute items (e.g., be sure parking passes are in place; snacks are ready, including plates, napkins, water cups; scrap paper is available, educational materials are in place for the first tutoring session, computers up and running; character-building portion of your first session is ready to go, etc.)

U. Say a prayer, welcome the students, and have a great tutoring session! Be sure to thank the Lord for a successful first session after it is completed!

Printed in the United States
By Bookmasters